My New Pet

Rabbit

Jinny Johnson

A⁺
Smart Apple Media

Published by Smart Apple Media,
an imprint of Black Rabbit Books
P.O. Box 3263, Mankato, Minnesota, 56002
www.blackrabbitbooks.com

Printed in the United States of America,
at Corporate Graphics in North Mankato, Minnesota.

Designed by Guy Callaby
Edited by Mary-Jane Wilkins
Illustrations by Bill Donohoe

Library of Congress Cataloging-in-Publication Data

Johnson, Jinny, 1949-
Rabbit / Jinny Johnson.
    p. cm. -- (My new pet)
Audience: K to grade 3.
Summary: "Describes life, features, and habits of pet
rabbits. Also helps child select a pet"-- Provided by
publisher.
Includes index.
ISBN 978-1-62588-028-4 (library binding)
1. Rabbits--Juvenile literature. I. Title.
SF453.2.J638 2014
636.932'2--dc23
                          2013002968

Photo acknowledgements
l = left, r = right, t = top, b = bottom
title page Masalski Maksim; 2 Vasyl Helevachuk; 3t Joy
Brown, b Eric Isselée, 6 Eric Isselée, 10 Maria Teijeiro,
11 Andris Tkacenko, 17 Eric Isselée, 18 Sompoch
Tangthai, 20 and 21 all Stefan Petru Andronache.
All images Shutterstock, except page 10 Thinkstock.
Front cover: ravl/Shutterstock

DAD0510
052013
9 8 7 6 5 4 3 2 1

Contents

I'm very excited. My mom says I can have a pet rabbit!

I want to know all about rabbits so I can look after my pet.

Here's what I have found out.

A **rabbit** has a plump, rounded body, long ears, and big eyes.

Rabbits are **good-tempered** and make great family pets. They are easily scared, so we must treat them very gently.

Pet rabbits usually live between **seven** and **ten** years.

Wild rabbits live in groups and shelter in burrows they dig in the ground.

A rabbit's coat should be smooth and shiny, with no bare patches.

Rabbits like **company** and we've decided to have two so they won't get lonely.

I will look for rabbits that have clean ears, bright eyes, and a clean nose. These show they are **healthy**.

Before
we get
my rabbits,
my dad
and I will buy a big **hutch**
and **bedding** to put inside.

The more room my rabbits
have, the healthier they will be.

We will buy **food bowls**, a **water bottle**, and a **grooming brush**.

I will keep my pets in the yard, but rabbits can live indoors, too. Indoor rabbits need a big cage with a plastic base and wire top. I might bring my rabbits indoors if it gets very cold.

I'm going to enjoy making my new pets' home ready.

They can hide and sleep in this area.

First I will line the floor of the hutch with **newspaper**.

Then I will put in some **wood shavings** to soak up the rabbits' pee.

I will put in **lots** of hay for them to snuggle up and sleep in.

I know it's very important to keep my pets clean.

Every day I will wash and dry their food bowls and wash and fill up their water bottle.

Every few days I will take out any wet or dirty bedding. I will sweep out any droppings, too.

Every week I will clean
out the hutch and put in
fresh bedding.

*Rabbits like being brushed.
Sit on the ground with your
rabbit and brush it gently.*

Rabbits feed on **plants** and they do not eat meat. They like to eat **hay** and should always have fresh hay in their hutch.

My mom and I will buy some dried food for my rabbits from the pet store to give them every day.

Rabbits like **fresh food**, too. I will give them treats such as carrots, celery, apples, and dandelion leaves. I won't give them lettuce. It's not good for rabbits.

I know I have to be very **gentle** with my new pets at first.

Everything will be strange to them and they might be **frightened**.

Rabbits love to chew. I will give mine chewing toys from the pet store so their teeth don't grow too long.

I will let them get used to their new home before I try to touch them.

Wild rabbits get plenty of **exercise** as they hop around looking for food.

Pet rabbits need exercise too, so I will let my pets out of their hutch every day to run around. I will **watch** them very carefully.

Pet rabbits like to play in cardboard tube tunnels or boxes with holes to run through.

Hurray! I have my new rabbits. They are both **female** and they are ten weeks old.

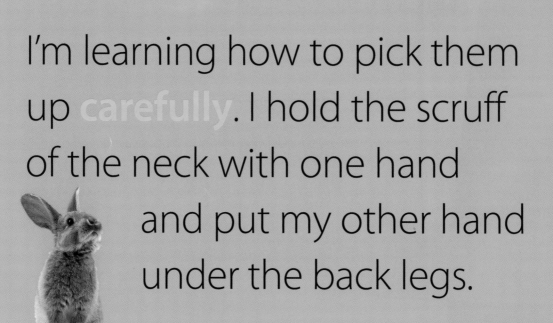

I'm learning how to pick them up **carefully**. I hold the scruff of the neck with one hand and put my other hand under the back legs.

I put my rabbit in its hutch back feet first in case it gets frightened and **kicks** me.

My new pets are going to be very happy—and so am I!

Notes for parents

Choosing a pet
Make sure you buy healthy rabbits from a good pet store or breeder. Take the animals to the vet for a health check. Ask the vet to check the sex of the animals too. Pet stores sometimes get it wrong!

Handling and caring for a rabbit
Show children how to handle a rabbit properly. Teach them to respect animals and always treat them gently.

Health
As a parent you need to make sure any pet is looked after properly. Supervise feeding and handling, especially at first. Keep an eye on the animal's health. Check its teeth and claws regularly and take the pet to the vet if they grow too long.

Words to remember

burrow
A hole dug in the ground where a wild rabbit makes its home.

hutch
A home for a pet rabbit. A hutch is usually made of wood and kept outside.

grooming
Caring for and cleaning the fur. You can buy special brushes for your rabbit.

scruff
The loose skin at the back of a rabbit's neck.

Index